Contents

What is a rescue boat?

A rescue boat, or lifeboat, is a boat that helps in **emergencies** at sea, on lakes and on rivers. Rescue boats are used for search and rescue (SAR). They help to find people in the water and carry them back to shore.

A US coastguard crew is called out to an emergency.

A rescue boat has a **crew** of people. They are trained to rescue people using the boat's equipment.

Offshore lifeboats

Some rescue boats can carry out rescue missions in bad weather. They are called **offshore** lifeboats. They are very fast.

This is a special lifeboat that is used in the UK. It is almost unsinkable.

If an offshore lifeboat is knocked over by a big wave, it will flip the right way again. This means it can go through huge waves.

Inside a rescue boat

In the cabin of a rescue boat are radio and **navigation** equipment. The crew can talk to their base and other boats. Even in bad weather, they can find their way to ships in trouble.

Using radio equipment to speak to people on the shore can help to save lives in an emergency.

This boat carries its own small **inflatable** rescue boat to use in shallow water.

Emergency!

When an emergency call comes, it is important for a rescue boat to act as fast as possible. The crew rushes to its boat and puts on special clothes – then it's time to launch.

Some boats are kept on water, ready for action. Others are kept on the shore.

This lifeboat is launched into the water by sliding down a ramp.

CROMER LIFEBOAT

Inshore lifeboats

An **inshore** lifeboat is a rescue boat that works close to the shore, or on lakes or rivers. Inshore boats are smaller than offshore boats. They can't go to sea in rough conditions.

Outboard motor

U.S. CO

Small lifeboats help to rescue people during floods.

Rubber tube

Inshore lifeboats are normally a type of boat called a rigid inflatable. They have a rubber tube around the edge.

Inshore lifeboats are powered by one or two big, powerful **outboard motors**.

Little lifesavers

Coastguards use all sorts of small craft for rescuing people close to the shore. **Jet boats** and **jet skis** are good in shallow water. They don't have **propellers** that could hit the seabed.

A **hovercraft** rescues people stuck in shallow water or mud.

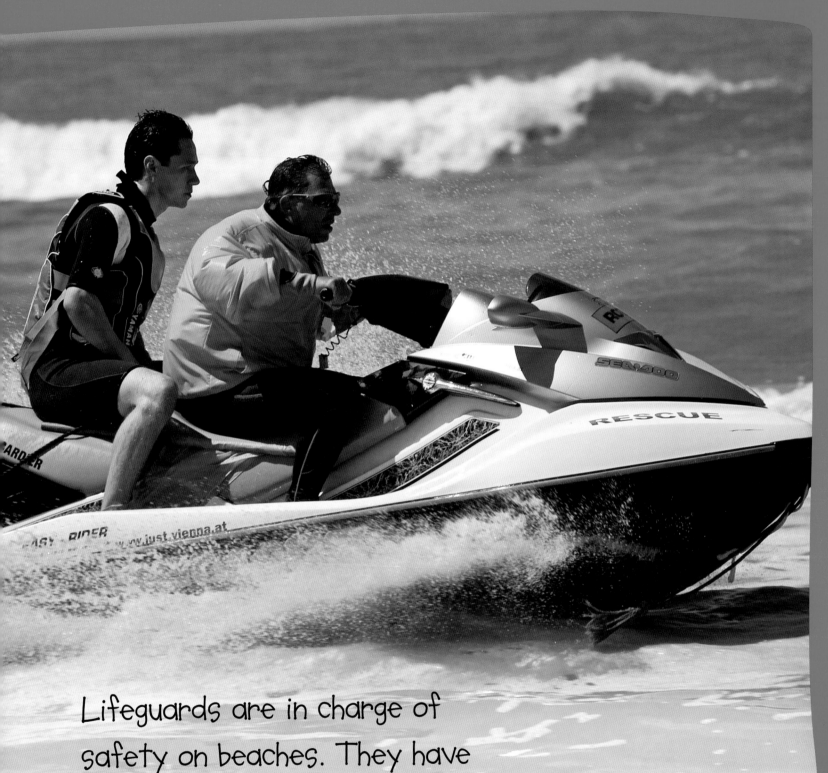

Lifeguards are in charge of safety on beaches. They have jet boats and jet skis to rescue injured surfers from the waves.

Jet skis are powered by a jet of water that comes out of the back.

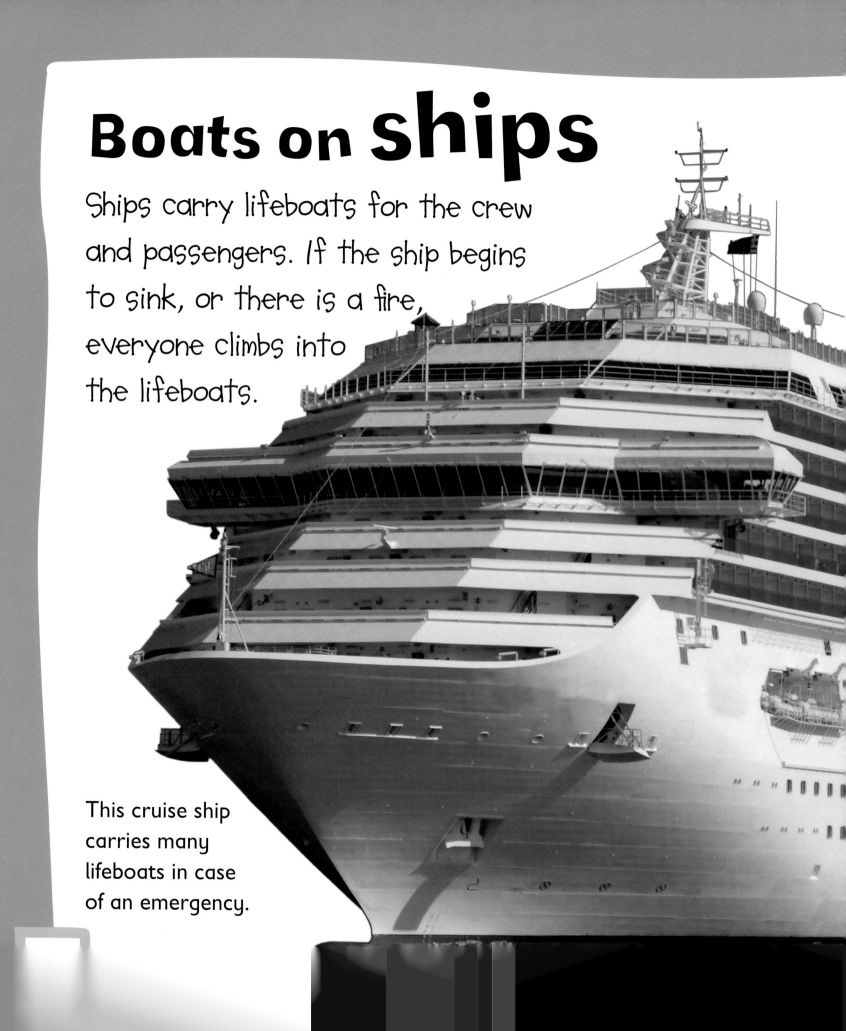

Boats on ships

Ships carry lifeboats for the crew and passengers. If the ship begins to sink, or there is a fire, everyone climbs into the lifeboats.

This cruise ship carries many lifeboats in case of an emergency.

Lots of people can travel to shore on a ship's lifeboat.

Each lifeboat carries important equipment for the people on board. This includes drinking water and medical supplies in case people are injured.

Big rescue boats

Some countries use rescue boats that are much bigger than normal lifeboats. The ships can stay at sea for many days, and the crew live on board.

This ship is called an ice breaker. It moves quickly and easily through icy water.

Ocean rescue boats have a landing pad for a rescue helicopter. The helicopter carries people to shore.

Crews often practise air-rescue missions.

Tugs

A tug is a large boat that is used to tow ships. It is a strong boat with powerful engines. Tugs often rescue ships that have broken down, and tow them to safety.

PANAMA

Tugs also help to fight fires on ships. They have hoses and powerful water **pumps** to spray water onto the flames.

This cargo ship is being pulled to safety by a tug boat.

Activities

- Which picture shows a hovercraft, an offshore lifeboat and a jet ski?

- Make a drawing of your favourite rescue boat. What sort of boat is it? Is it large or small? What colour is it?

- Write a story about the rescue mission you would most like to go on. It could be anywhere in the world – or even on another planet! Where would you like to go? Who would you have to rescue? How dangerous would it be? How long would it take?

- Which of these rescue boats would be used in icy water?

Glossary

Crew
The people who work on a ship or boat.

Emergency
A dangerous situation that must be dealt with straight away.

Hovercraft
A vehicle that skims across water or land on an air-filled cushion.

Inflatable
Something that can be blown up with air, such as a balloon.

Inshore
Close to the shore.

Jet boat
A boat that is pushed along by a jet of water at the back.

Jet ski
A small boat, like a motorbike on water, pushed along by a jet of water at the back.

Navigation
Finding the way.

Offshore
Far out to sea, a long way from the shore.

Outboard motor
An engine attached to the back of a boat.

Propeller
A piece of equipment with blades that spin around to make a ship or boat move.

Pump
A machine that sucks and pushes water along hoses.

Index